Pocket law guide

Unmarried Couples and the Law

www.tesco.com

LAWPACK

Pocket law guide

Unmarried Couples and the Law

by Philippa Pearson

The author

Philippa Pearson is a partner at Family Law in Partnership, in London, solicitors who specialise in family law.

Unmarried Couples and the Law
by Philippa Pearson

Published by
Lawpack Publishing Limited
76–89 Alscot Road
London SE1 3AW

www.lawpack.co.uk

ISBN: 1 904053 59 9

Printed in Great Britain

The law is stated as at 1 June 2004

Valid in England and Wales

Exclusion of Liability and Disclaimer

While every effort has been made to ensure that this Lawpack Pocket Law Guide provides accurate and expert guidance, it is impossible to predict all the circumstances in which it may be used. Accordingly, neither the publisher, author, retailer nor any other suppliers shall be liable to any person or entity with respect to any loss or damage caused or alleged to be caused by the information contained in or omitted from this Lawpack Pocket Law Guide.

For convenience (and for no other reason), 'him', 'he' and 'his' have been used throughout and should be read to include 'her', 'she' and 'her'.

Contents

	Some facts and figures	vii
	Introduction	ix
1	**Things to consider when you decide to live together**	1
2	**Children**	17
3	**Domestic violence**	27
4	**Splitting up**	33
5	**Gay and lesbian rights**	41
6	**Benefits and taxation**	45
	Appendices	49
	Index	69

Some facts and figures

There has been a large increase in people living together in Great Britain over the last 20 years. Among non-married men and women under 60, the proportion of people living together has more than doubled during the period 1986 to 2002 (from 13 to 28 per cent for women and from 12 to 25 per cent for men).

This rise has been accompanied by a shift in attitudes towards marriage and living together. The British Social Attitudes Survey of 2002 revealed that attitudes towards partnerships differed with age. More than four-fifths of 18- to 44-year-olds agreed or strongly agreed that 'it's all right for a couple to live together without intending to get married'; whereas only half this number agreed in the 65 or over category. Only 14 per cent of 18- to 24-year-olds believed that 'married people were generally happier than unmarried people', compared to 43 per cent of those aged 65 or over.

These attitudes are reflective of figures that show that most people who live together are aged 30–34. Between the ages of 20 and 49, an average of 32 per cent of the non-married population choose to live together, but after the age of 50, this drops below 20 per cent.

According to the General Household Survey (2001), among women who were living together with their partner/spouse and were between 16 and 59, 51 per cent of married women compared to 37 per cent of non-married women had at least one dependent child living with them.

Introduction

Human beings thrive on living together. As Pooh Bear put it, 'it's so much better with two'. Or is it? If a live-in relationship goes wrong because of separation, illness or death, many complex problems can arise and unfortunately, more often than not, the law does not help. So it is important to protect yourself and your loved ones by taking the right steps before they occur.

There are many myths about the law relating to those who live together which give people a false sense of security. The most common myth is that a relationship is protected in law by virtue of it being a 'common law marriage'. But there are no such people as 'common law wives' and 'common law husbands', since the concept of a common law marriage was abolished way back in 1753 by the Marriage Act. Despite the fact that it is frequently referred to in the press, it plays no part in the law of England and Wales (although there is something similar in Scotland, which is outside the scope of this book).

If you are a couple living together unmarried therefore, you may not have any special rights against your partner if you separate, however long you have lived together and however many children you may have. This means that you may have no special rights for financial help if things go wrong. But there are steps you can take to ensure that you will be financially provided for in the event of separation, illness or death. This book will help you to take those steps and if you are one of the many people who did not take any of these steps when your relationship was going well, then do not despair. This book will tell you how to make the most of the law and about the protection you may be able to find.

CHAPTER 1

Things to consider when you decide to live together

In the excitement of moving in together, the last thing you want to think about is the legal issues, but it is always best to know where you stand in the event of your relationship coming to an end. Even if you have lived with your partner for years and have children, you may still have no rights at all, so it is wise to consider your position from the outset.

The various issues you should think about, which are discussed in this chapter, are as follows:

- Who owns your home?
- Do you have rights over each other's finances?
- Do you want to make decisions on your lifestyle?
- What happens if one of you falls ill?
- What happens if one of you dies?

It is also worthwhile making formal agreements on these issues so that conflict can be avoided if any disputes arise. To live together without doing so could leave you or your family in a very vulnerable or uncertain position if one of you dies or you split up, whether or not you are the one with good income or most of the capital in your relationship.

The agreements you should think about preparing are:

1. A trust deed relating to the ownership of your property.

2. A cohabitation agreement dealing with the financial structure of your relationship.
3. A living together agreement on how you run your life.
4. An Enduring Power of Attorney in case either of you becomes incapacitated.
5. Mutual Wills, where each of you makes a Will to leave your interest in assets (e.g. property, bank account and any other assets you see fit) to the other, together with whatever other provisions may be appropriate.
6. A parental responsibility agreement if you have children.

Most of these agreements are explained in this chapter and the parental responsibility agreement is discussed in chapter 2. A few sample agreements can also be found in the Appendix at the end of this book.

Who owns your home?

There are two ways of owning a property. The first way is 'legally': the legal owner of a property has his name registered as the owner on the property's title deeds or at the Land Registry.

The other way of owning a property is 'beneficially'. Beneficial ownership arises under what is called the 'law of equity', which is where the court looks beyond who actually owns the property, but instead considers the question of who should be said to own an interest in a property. Although the beneficial owner's name may not appear on any of the deeds or at the Land Registry, a court may consider that a beneficial owner is still entitled to a certain percentage of the value in a property. This may be because he has worked on the property to enhance its value or has paid money towards it.

The law of equity is very complex and in some circumstances where people think that they should have an interest in a property, the law of equity cannot help; for example, where they have paid the mortgage interest but not made payments towards the capital borrowing or, in some circumstances, where they have contributed money to the general household expenses rather than to the property itself.

If you think you have a right to an interest in a property, take advice from a solicitor with experience in cohabitation law to find out if you have such an interest and how difficult it may be to claim it through the legal system.

Moving into a property owned by one of you

Moving in with the legal owner of a property gives you no legal rights over your partner's property. Legal ownership can only be transferred to you formally by way of a transfer, on a form issued by the Land Registry called a TR1, and with the consent of the mortgage lender (if there is one).

? Do I have any right to stay if my partner tries to kick me out of his property?

This will depend on the circumstances, so you should speak to a specialist solicitor straight away.

The only other way of obtaining rights over a property (through beneficial ownership) is for the two of you to reach an agreement and enter into a 'trust deed' (for which you should consult a solicitor – see below for further details).

If you are neither a legal owner nor have a trust deed, but you believe that you have acted to your disadvantage or relied on a mistaken belief or promise that you would have an interest in the property, it may be possible for you to establish a beneficial interest under the law of equity but, as we said before, proving this can be difficult.

The most common position you will find yourself in is that you will have no beneficial or legal entitlement to the property at all. Indeed, you may only be occupying the property by what is known as a 'bare licence', which means that if the owner asks you to leave, you must do so as you have no legal rights to be there. However, this can place you in a very vulnerable position so always take legal advice before you pack your bags, particularly if you have a child.

Renting together

Point of Law

Family Law Act 1996

If you are both renting a property and the tenancy is held in one of your names or in joint names, the court may have the power to transfer the tenancy into the other cohabitant's name or just one name when you split up. This application is usually made when the separating parties cannot agree into whose name the tenancy should be transferred and is best handled by a solicitor. If there are children, the parent who is to have the day-to-day care of the children will normally have the tenancy transferred to him. If there are no children, the court will decide the case on its merits.

Buying together

When you decide to buy a property together, make sure that your conveyancing solicitor discusses with you at the outset whether you should own the property as 'joint tenants' or 'tenants in common'. The distinction is extremely important.

Joint tenants

If you own the property as joint tenants, this means that you will each have an equal interest in the property and if one of you dies before the other, the share of the deceased will pass automatically to the survivor under the principle known as 'the right of survivorship' and not according to the deceased's Will (whatever it may say) or the law that applies to those who die without a Will, called 'the law of intestacy' (see below for further information).

Tenants in common

If you own a property as tenants in common, you do not necessarily have equal shares. You may think this is appropriate if you have made unequal contributions towards the purchase price and want this to be reflected on the sale of the property. Owning as a tenant in common also means that your shares are separate from each other, which means that if one of you dies before the other, the share of the deceased does not pass automatically to the survivor, but instead passes according to the wishes of the deceased's Will or the law of intestacy as appropriate.

If you intend to hold the property as tenants in common, you should discuss with your conveyancer whether you should enter into a trust deed. He can draft one for you.

A trust deed

A trust deed is a binding agreement regarding your property which means that you can sue your partner if he breaches it. It is important that it deals with all the issues that may arise in relation to the property if you separate or if one of you dies.

It is not the same as a cohabitation agreement (see below) since it only deals with the property and not with other aspects of your relationship. The property issues must be dealt with in a separate document (trust deed) because the cohabitation agreement may include some less important clauses that a court will not want to enforce. Problems could arise because if the court happened to ignore certain clauses in it, there is a risk that it may disregard the arrangements you have made elsewhere in the agreement about the property. Since the agreement regarding your property is likely to be the most important aspect of any arrangements you have, it is always advisable that you have a separate trust deed.

The usual issues dealt with in a trust deed are as follows:

- The exact percentage of your beneficial interest in the property (i.e. what your shares in the property are to be in the event of death or separation).
- What is to happen in the event that your relationship breaks down. Will one of you be allowed to buy out the other one and in what circumstances?
- How is the value of the property to be calculated in these circumstances? Will one of you be allowed to vacate the

property and if so, for how long should that person continue to be responsible for the mortgage and the outgoings on the property? At what point will the person left in occupation have to take these over?

- Under what circumstances should the property be sold?
- What do you intend to happen to the property in the event of death?
- Who is to pay the outgoings relating to the property (e.g. buildings insurance and repairs)? Will this be affected by the birth of a child?
- How will you agree the method by which improvements, repairs, etc. will be carried out?
- How will you take into account any failure to pay any of the items referred to in the trust deed, i.e. will there be a recalculation of your respective beneficial interests in the property?
- Any other issues you consider may be important that relate to the property.

Do you have rights over each other's finances?

Joint bank accounts and credit cards

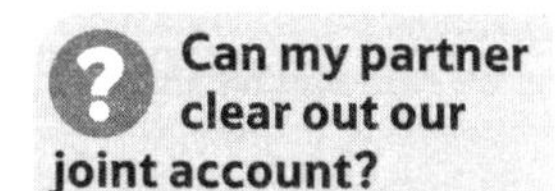

Can my partner clear out our joint account?

Any money put into a joint account is treated as jointly owned so either of you can remove it at any time, even if one of you put in more money than the other.

You may decide to open up a joint bank account when you start living together. If you do, you should be aware that once any money is invested in the account, it is treated as jointly owned and either of you can, at any time, remove all or part of that money. This rule applies even if one of you has put in far more money than the other. If you are not happy to be caught by this rule, you should instruct the bank (usually together) not to accept cheques/cashpoint withdrawals by one of you alone in excess of an agreed figure (say £250).

If at any time you become concerned that the account may be abused by the other account holder, it is usually sufficient to tell the bank and it will then prevent any further transactions taking place on the account without your joint authority.

The law of equity states that items purchased from joint money belong to the person who purchases them, unless they were obviously for the other person's use or they were joint purchases. Do keep this in mind when big purchases are being made as it may be a good idea to go and buy them together!

You should bear in mind that any debt owing on a jointly owned card or account is legally treated as belonging to both of the owners 'jointly and severally'. This means that the bank or the credit card/store card company can pursue both of you for the debt or just one of you for the whole debt. This can of course be particularly unfair if you are the one being chased for the debt when it was run up by your partner.

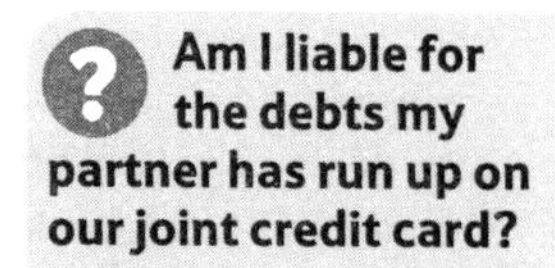

Am I liable for the debts my partner has run up on our joint credit card?

Yes. Your bank or credit card company can chase both of you or just one of you for the whole debt.

If you have any doubts at all about your partner's ability to control his spending, you must ensure that strict limitations are put in place for your debts and overdraft so that the level of indebtedness cannot get out of hand. Better still, make sure in these circumstances that you are each responsible for your own debts by having no overdraft on your joint account and by possibly having separate credit/store cards.

If your partner dies, the money held in a joint bank account will go to you under the principle of law known as the 'right of survivorship'. It will not pass into his estate and then be distributed to his beneficiaries. Likewise, any jointly owned debt will pass to you (something you may wish to avoid!) so again it may be best to have separate credit/store cards.

The cohabitation agreement

A cohabitation agreement can be drawn up between you to record the financial obligations you wish to have towards each other in order to avoid dispute. It should cover the following:

- Who is to pay the outgoings (electricity/water bills, etc.)?
- How will home repairs and improvements be agreed?
- How will those repairs and improvements be funded?
- What will be the circumstances in which the home is sold? (These can be more detailed than the provisions you would put in your trust deed, since it could deal with such things as how old the children may have to be or how many of them should be living at home.)
- How will the joint accounts be operated?
- How will the joint credit cards be operated?
- What are your intentions regarding your estate? (Wills would still be required, but the agreement can be important evidence if it shows that it was agreed that certain terms would be included in a Will.)
- Who is responsible for any school fees?
- Will you each enter into an Enduring Power of Attorney or a Living Will (see below)?
- How will your possessions be divided?

Only legal issues should be contained in a cohabitation agreement, but they may not be upheld by the courts because they are not necessarily binding under English law. However, they will always be good evidence for the court if there is a disagreement between a couple and legal action follows. A simple template agreement is included in the Appendix; this is meant as a guide only and you are advised to take legal advice before drawing up your own.

Reviewing the cohabitation agreement

As time goes on, your relationship will change and significant things may happen in your life that may make the terms of the cohabitation agreement unfair. If a cohabitation agreement is clearly unjust, it is unlikely it will be upheld by the courts. Therefore if anything substantial does happen in your relationship, it is wise to consider redrafting the cohabitation agreement; such a reason may be:

- the birth of a child;
- one of you becomes seriously ill;
- one of you becomes disabled;
- one of you is made redundant;
- a significant change in your financial circumstances or the financial contributions you each make towards your relationship and your home;
- one of you receives a large inheritance.

Remember that if you decide to marry, the cohabitation agreement will not be treated as being a prenuptial agreement. In this instance it will only provide evidence of what your intentions were towards each other when you were living together. This is because marriage is itself a contract and it supersedes any pre-existing contract.

Do you want to make decisions on your lifestyle?

Some couples who decide to live together choose to enter into a living together agreement. This is a document in which the couple can record any moral or lifestyle issues that are non-legal so that each party is clear as to what is expected of them from the outset. This can then prevent disputes arising over matters that are outside the compass of the law.

In a living together agreement you can deal with the following issues:

- Who is to have responsibility for cleaning the home?

- Who is to have responsibility for cooking for the family?
- How are the children to be brought up?
- What religious upbringing or type of schooling should they have?
- Who will you both turn to in the event of relationship difficulties (e.g. to Relate, the relationship counselling service or to a faith)?
- Any other issues that may be important to the two of you and which you think need regulation.

Specialist family solicitors or mediators can draft living together agreements for you, but couples can also prepare their own since they are not intended to be legally binding.

An example of a simple agreement is included in the Appendix at the end of this book.

What happens if one of you falls ill?

An Enduring Power of Attorney

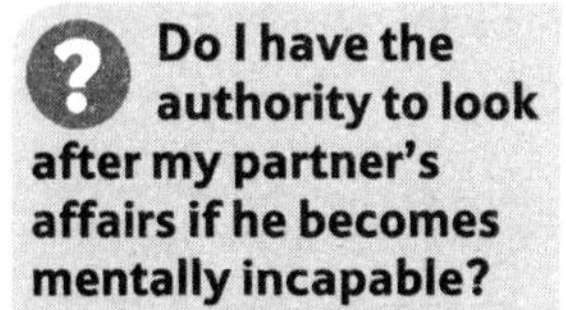

There is always the possibility that either you or your partner may become mentally incapable as a result of illness or an accident. If you are married, it is unlikely that anybody would question your spouse dealing with your affairs, but if you are not, your partner may not automatically be viewed as your 'representative' and it is therefore wise in these circumstances to draw up a formal document known as an Enduring Power of Attorney (EPA). This authorises your partner to act on your behalf in all matters concerning your property and affairs should you become mentally incapable, but it does not grant him the power to make decisions regarding your medical care.

It is absolutely vital that you trust the person to whom you give an EPA because if you are deemed to be mentally incapable, you will not be able to unappoint him if you become dissatisfied with the way in which he is acting on your behalf.

A General Power of Attorney

A General Power of Attorney (GPA) is similar to an EPA, but it authorises someone to do specific acts rather than to act on your behalf generally. You may use it, for example, to authorise someone to sign certain documents on your behalf, or use your bank account to make certain payments, while you are out of the country or in hospital.

Unlike an EPA, a GPA is automatically annulled (i.e. no longer valid) if you become mentally incapable so this is an advantage if you wish to restrict your representative's authority. The only disadvantage is that it may not give him all of the powers that he requires if you become mentally incapable and it will be left to the Court of Protection to deal with some matters on your behalf. The Court of Protection is a special court which deals solely with the issues arising out of the affairs of those who are incapable of managing their own.

The meaning of 'next of kin' and 'hospital proxies'

It is not clear under the law whether your unmarried partner is your next of kin (i.e. the person who can make decisions for you when you are incapable, usually your nearest relative) when it comes to giving instructions regarding your medical treatment. This can be a problem, particularly when there are other family members competing for the role of next of kin or representative, such as the first family (i.e. the children from a first marriage).

Fortunately, there is a legal principle known as the 'doctrine of necessity' that justifies medical intervention in an emergency when it is not appropriate to obtain the consent of the next of kin. However, a partner can still encounter difficulties with the medical profession when the other partner is ill, particularly if their relationship has been one of short duration.

To get round this, it is possible to provide a hospital with written documents declaring which person is to be your next of kin. This has no legal effect, but it can be used as evidence if there is any dispute as to whom is to have this authority. All you need to do is ask your hospital to provide a 'healthcare proxy appointment form' and in it you can give precise details of exactly what medical decisions can be taken by the proxy. Sometimes these can be attached to a Living Will (see below).

? Is my partner seen as my 'next of kin' when it comes to my medical treatment?

The law is unclear on this matter. As a result, you can fill in a 'healthcare proxy appointment form', which will inform the hospital of your medical decisions.

Living Wills

Any patient who is suffering from a terminal illness can unwittingly cause disputes between relatives and partners if it is not clear what is to happen about his medical treatment in the event that he becomes incapacitated. A Living Will is a document that can be used to avoid such conflicts as in it a person can state clearly in what circumstances a life support machine can be turned off and where he would like to die (e.g. at home or in hospital).

What happens if one of you dies?

In the event that a partner in a couple living together dies, the law that applies to them is very different from the law relating to married couples. First, the surviving partner will have no right to claim a widow's pension unless a specific nomination to that effect has been made and accepted by the trustees of the pension fund. Furthermore, the surviving partner will not necessarily have any rights over his partner's estate (i.e. his property, money and belongings).

By law, if one spouse in a married couple leaves a Will in which he excludes the other spouse or leaves an inadequate amount of money, then the surviving spouse can make an application to the court to adjust the Will so that he receives sufficient money from the estate of the deceased.

Also, if a married person dies, but has not made a Will, the law of intestacy will apply and his spouse will automatically receive a large part of his estate. The law of intestacy is a fixed set of rules relating to how an estate should be distributed in the event that no Will is left.

> **Point of Law**
>
> *Inheritance (Provision for Family and Dependants) Act 1975*

In contrast, if your live-in partner dies and he does not leave a Will or in his Will he leaves you insufficient money, then you can apply for monies out of his estate *only* if:

1. you were financially dependent upon him at the time of death; and/or
2. you had been living with your partner for a continuous period of at least two years immediately prior to the date of death.

To be successful on an application made under either of the above, you have to have good evidence to support either 1. or 2. and it can be a good idea to refer to a cohabitation agreement if there is one because this should have evidence as to what was intended.

The law of intestacy

If someone dies without making a Will, he dies 'intestate'. The law of intestacy states the following:

1. The total estate goes to a surviving spouse where there are no children, parents, brothers or sisters.
2. If the deceased is survived by a spouse and children, the

spouse will get the 'chattels' (i.e. personal possessions) and a fixed sum (currently £125,000). In addition, the spouse will have the right to use one half of the remaining estate for the rest of his life and on his death it will then pass to the deceased's children. The remaining half-share goes directly to any children.

3. If there is a surviving spouse and a parent or brothers and sisters but no children, it is the same as for number 2 above but the fixed sum received by the surviving spouse is increased to £200,000.
4. The total estate passes to the children of the deceased if there is no surviving spouse.
5. If there is no surviving spouse or children, the estate passes to the blood relatives of the deceased in order of closeness, starting with his parents.

So if you and your partner were not married, his estate will not pass to you automatically, however long your relationship may have lasted. It is therefore particularly important that you both make Wills. If you do not, then under the law of intestacy you may receive no money at all.

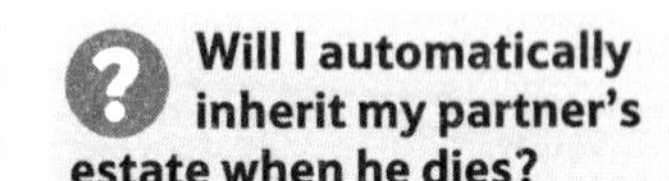

Will I automatically inherit my partner's estate when he dies?

No, so you must both make Wills. If your partner dies without making a Will, his estate will be distributed among his blood relatives in accordance with the rules of intestacy.

Children

If you die and you have a child who is born outside marriage, he will be treated by the law in exactly the same way as the child of a married couple. This means that if he does not receive sufficient inheritance under a Will, he can make an application (using an adult who brings the application for him as his 'next friend') against your estate simply by virtue of being your child and if there is no Will, he is automatically entitled under the law of intestacy as can be seen above.

Making a Will

The law has precise rules about the way you should make your Will. There is a wide range of DIY Will kits, books, forms and software to help you, all available online at www.tesco.com/legalstore.

CHAPTER 2

Children

Registering your child's birth

Point of Law

Births and Deaths Registration Act 1953

If you are unmarried, as the natural mother you can register a child's birth without the natural father being present. However, you cannot place the father's name on the birth certificate without the father also attending the registry. The law states that:

'the registrar cannot enter the name of any person as father of a child except at the joint request of the mother and the person stating himself to be the father of the child (in which case that person shall sign the register together with the mother) or at the request of the mother who brings with her a statutory declaration by the person who is the father of the child.'

A statutory declaration is a simple legal document which can be easily obtained from a solicitor.

If, at the time of the child's birth, the father is not registered, the father's name can be added later on. The law states that the birth can be re-registered:

- at the joint request of the mother and father;
- at the request of the mother if she provides a statutory declaration by the father;

- at the request of the father if he declares he is the father and the mother provides a statutory declaration that he is;
- by the mother providing a copy of a parental responsibility agreement they have both signed or a copy of a parental responsibility order made by the court; or
- by the mother or the father if certain other financial orders for the child have been made against the father.

Point of Law

Human Fertilisation and Embryology Act 1990

Where the couple have had IVF and the man is treated as the father of the child, his name can also be added to the register.

Putting the father's name on a birth certificate is a legal recognition by the father of his paternity of the child. It does not make any difference in relation to his legal obligations towards the child (e.g. child support). In other words, a natural father who is placed on the birth certificate is every bit as responsible for the child as one who is not registered.

Child law

Point of Law

Children Act 1989

The general principle of child law is that the child's welfare shall be the court's 'paramount consideration' when any court makes decisions regarding:

1. the upbringing of the child; or
2. the administration of the child's property (meaning how to manage, say, a house that has been left to a child or the application of any income arising from it).

When the court is asked to consider any issues in relation to the child, any other factors, such as the child's wishes or his emotional relationship with his brothers and sisters, are only relevant to the extent that they assist the court in determining the best solution for that child. It goes without saying therefore that, like the court, any decisions you make for your children should always have their best interests in mind.

One of the most important aspects of the law concerning the children of unmarried couples is parental responsibility.

What is parental responsibility?

The law describes parental responsibility as giving the parents all the 'rights, duties, powers, responsibilities and authority which by law a parent has in relation to a child and his property'.

The practical effect of parental responsibility is that where two parents have parental responsibility, one parent cannot make decisions about the child without the other parent agreeing the matter with him. If this is not possible, then either parent (although it is usually the parent who feels his wishes are being ignored) must apply to the court for the court to decide the issues. The types of issue that are covered by parental responsibility are major (as opposed to day-to-day) issues regarding a child, such as his education, religious instruction and medical care.

Why is it important to share parental responsibility?

If you do not share parental responsibility, then the mother (who always has parental responsibility automatically) can make important decisions regarding the child without the consent of the father. In these circumstances, if the father does not agree with the mother's actions, he can apply to the court for an order to overturn the mother's decision and for him to be granted parental responsibility (using Form C1 available from any County court – see Appendix). Usually, the order he needs will either be a prohibited steps order or a specific issue order (see below for further information).

Sometimes this process can be slow; depending on which court is hearing the application it may take weeks, even months, for a father's application for parental responsibility to be dealt with, making it difficult for the father to be successful on his other, more important applications because by then the mother has already acted on her decision. However, if the father automatically has parental responsibility, sometimes his application can be dealt with more quickly and he can stand a better chance of success on his other applications.

Another practical effect of only one parent having parental responsibility is that this parent can take the child out of the jurisdiction of England and Wales without the other parent's consent. This means that the parent is not guilty of any criminal offence if he takes the child to live in another country, and it can then be very difficult or even impossible for the other parent to obtain the return of the child to the jurisdiction. However, if the parents share parental responsibility and one parent takes the child out of the jurisdiction without the other parent's consent, the parent who removed the child is guilty of the criminal offence of child abduction. This can be a very serious matter. The international police organisation Interpol is often involved in the return of abducted children and where a child has been abducted to a Hague Convention country (i.e. countries which have signed the Hague Convention and have agreed to co-operate with each other in the area of child abduction) the child can often be returned to the UK within days or weeks.

Point of Law

Child Abduction Act 1984

Please note that England and Wales is a separate jurisdiction from Scotland and Northern Ireland and the moving of a child to Scotland or Northern Ireland can also be treated as child abduction if the consent of both parents with parental responsibility is not obtained.

Children born to unmarried parents

Any married couple who have a child automatically share equal parental responsibility but the situation is rather different for a couple who are not. If your child was born before 1 December 2003, only the mother has automatic parental responsibility. The natural father of that child can only gain parental responsibility by either:

- entering into a parental responsibility agreement;
- obtaining a court order giving him parental responsibility;
- marrying the mother.

> **If I don't have parental responsibility, do I still have to pay child support?**
>
> *Yes. The Child Support Agency assesses all fathers in the same way.*

If the mother with parental responsibility dies, the unmarried surviving father still does not gain automatic parental responsibility unless he has a court order, a parental responsibility agreement in his favour, or he was registered as the father of a child born after 1 December 2003. While an unmarried father of a child born before 1 December 2003 has no automatic parental responsibility for that child under the law, when it comes to providing financial support for the child the law makes no distinction between him and a father with parental responsibility. The Child Support Agency, for instance, will assess fathers without parental responsibility for child support in the same way it does for all other fathers and the court will allow an application to be made on behalf of a child for a lump sum to be paid by the father who does not have parental responsibility.

> Point of Law
>
> *Adoption and Children Act 2002*

Parents, whether or not they are married, share parental responsibility for a child born after 1 December 2003, providing that the father is registered on the birth certificate.

Entering into a parental responsibility agreement

A parental responsibility agreement is a legal document signed by both parents of a child when they are unmarried. Only the natural parents can sign a parental responsibility agreement. If you are not a biological parent and you wish to obtain parental responsibility for a child, then this can be gained only by way of an adoption order or a residence order from the court (see below). One exception to this is where a child has been conceived through the donation of sperm. Where an unmarried couple receive this service from a licensed practitioner, the male partner, rather than the donor, will be treated as the father of the child and will therefore be able to sign a parental responsibility agreement.

A parental responsibility agreement lasts until the child's 18th birthday or until revoked by an order of the court. However, a court only revokes an agreement in very rare circumstances.

In order to obtain parental responsibility, the parents must both sign the agreement, which can be obtained from a local County court (or from the Court Service website at www.courtservice.gov.uk) which they must then attend together in order to lodge it. The following documents need to be brought to the court by the parents as proof of identity (as well as a copy of the child's birth certificate by the mother).

Preferred evidence:
- Passport
- Photocard
- Student card

Acceptable evidence:
- DSS/benefits book
- Child benefit book
- Driving licence
- Sports/membership card (preferably with a photograph)
- Work/security pass (preferably with a photograph)
- Banker's card
- Firearms licence
- Prison number

If the parents have been identified in a court case concerning the child, there is no need for them to produce identification as long as there is a covering letter explaining the circumstances and at what court the hearing was held and the case number.

When a parental responsibility agreement is taken to court, the clerk who deals with the matter checks the agreement for the child's surname. If it differs from the name of both parents (e.g. the mother has married another man and taken his name), then this will be queried and proof must be given as to why the child has been given this surname. Otherwise, the child can have either the mother's or the father's surname, or a combination of the two.

The agreement form must be fully completed. Any 'care of' address must be explained and a solicitor's address will not be accepted.

After the check has been made by the clerk of the court, the clerk will ask to see a proof of identity as listed above. If no evidence is produced, then the agreement cannot be witnessed by the clerk and will not be valid.

Parents can only sign the agreement in the presence of the court clerk who witnesses it. The clerk has to check that they are the natural parents, and will complete the certificate of witness and sign and date the agreement, entering the address and court stamp. After doing this, the clerk will return the agreement to the parents for them to send to the Principal Registry of the Family Division where it will be registered.

It is possible for parents to attend any County court to sign a parental agreement, but it can only be registered at the Principal Registry.

If you have any further queries about parental responsibility agreements, you are advised to contact the Children's Section of the Principal Registry listed in the 'Useful contacts' section.

If things go wrong

If you are unable to agree on issues concerning your children with your partner, the first thing you should do is try to negotiate with your partner and a third party with a view to reaching an agreement. You may do this by making an appointment to see either a mediator (contactable through the UK College of Family Mediators or the Solicitors Family Law Association – see 'Useful contacts' for details) or a child psychologist (contactable through the British Association of Psychotherapists). If it is not possible for you to reach a negotiated agreement in this way, you may have no alternative but to make an application to the court.

The types of order that a court can make in relation to a child on an application by either parent are:

- parental responsibility orders;
- residence orders;
- contact orders;
- prohibited steps orders;
- specific issue orders.

Forms with which you can apply for these orders are available from your local County court or from www.courtservice.gov.uk.

The law makes it clear that a court should not make any order unless it is necessary (known as the principle of 'no order'). In other words, if the parents agree on how their child should be brought up and all the other arrangements for his welfare, the court will not intervene and will not be used to confirm their agreement; it will only interfere if the parents are in dispute. As the child gets older and becomes more able to make his own decisions, the court will take more notice of the child's views on an issue. While these views can be important, however, they will not be binding upon the court.

The age at which a child can make a reasoned decision differs with each child but, generally, the court will consider a child's views from the age of nine and will begin to take them more seriously from around the age of 12. Regarding medical intervention, the case of Victoria Gillick (in relation to the prescription of the contraceptive pill to children under the age of 16) established that children who are under 16 may obtain medical assistance without the consent of their parents, providing it can be shown that they are of sufficient age and understanding. In any event, any child over the age of 16 can obtain medical treatment without the consent of a parent or guardian.

? What can I do if I don't agree with the mother of my child regarding our child's upbringing?

If you don't have parental responsibility, you should try to negotiate with her, perhaps through a mediator, and, if that fails, you can apply to the court for parental responsibility (if you don't already have it) and an order to overturn her decisions.

Parental responsibility orders

While court orders can be obtained to give fathers parental responsibility, the process of getting one can be costly in both emotional and financial terms. If you are in agreement that both of you should hold parental responsibility, the best and simplest way of dealing with this is to sign a parental responsibility agreement. Draft agreements can be obtained from County courts or from www.courtservice.gov.uk.

Residence orders

'Residence order' is the name now used which has replaced the old 'custody order' and is the type of order that a court will make when it is necessary for the court to decide where a child should live. A residence order can be made in favour of one parent or in favour of both parents (then known as a 'joint residence order'). Joint residence orders used to be relatively rare because the courts considered that a child would benefit from having one main base, but their popularity is on the increase.

Contact orders

'Contact' is the legal term now used instead of the old 'access order'. It is used to refer to the time when the parent who does not have the day-to-day care of the children can see them. It is usual for parents to agree on the arrangements for contact between them but if they cannot, a court may make an order for contact. Contact can include overnight (also known as 'staying') contact or even supervised contact where it is appropriate that the child should not be left alone with a particular parent.

Certain third parties (e.g. grandparents and step-parents) can also apply for contact with a child, although, in the first instance, they have to ask permission for 'leave' of the court to bring their application in Form C1. Such permission is usually granted.

Prohibited steps orders

This can be applied for if it is necessary to obtain an order to prevent something happening in relation to the child (e.g. to prevent him from having contact with an undesirable person or to stop a parent from taking him to a particular place or sending him to a particular school).

Specific issue orders

A court will make this for any other issue relating to a child that is not covered by residence, contact or prohibited steps orders. They are usually orders made by a court when it is asked to make a decision about an important aspect of the child's life (e.g. a particular school a child should attend). One situation in which this kind of order may be needed would be if you wish to take your child to live in another country.

CHAPTER 3

Domestic violence

Point of Law

Family Law Act 1996

Violence within the home occurs with alarming frequency. In 2001/02, the British Crime Survey found that there were an estimated 635,000 incidents of domestic violence in England and Wales. The majority of victims are women (around 81 per cent).

Until relatively recently, the law was often reluctant to intervene, but a growing appreciation among police officers of the terrifying nature of domestic violence and a change of law have meant that it has become much easier for victims to seek the protection of the law. However, many victims have still felt unable to take proceedings against the perpetrators of the violence all the way through the courts. This has been for a variety of reasons, such as being pressurised by the perpetrator or by family to drop the proceedings.

As a result, the recent changes in the law now allow the police to prosecute a perpetrator of domestic violence without needing the ongoing co-operation of the victim. The law is also currently undergoing change in order to give the courts more effective powers against offenders. For details of the new law, which is covered by the Domestic Violence Bill, see below.

Non-molestation orders or orders to prevent harassment, violence or threats of violence

At the time of going to press, the law states that if you live together or you used to live together (which means those who live in the same house as each other but not where one is an employee of the other, such as an au pair and his employer, and are not tenants, lodgers or boarders) and you are subjected to, or threatened with, violence or harassment, you can obtain a non-molestation order. This is an injunction (i.e. a court order preventing a person from taking action), which if breached can lead to the imprisonment of the harasser.

The definition of molestation is wide and it includes such actions as following somebody, telephoning him repeatedly and sending notes through his door, etc.

Both heterosexual and same-sex couples are entitled to obtain non-molestation orders. For legal advice on how to obtain one, contact the Law Society (see the 'Useful contacts' section for its details). In the event of an emergency, telephone the police.

Occupation orders or orders to exclude someone from a property or part of it

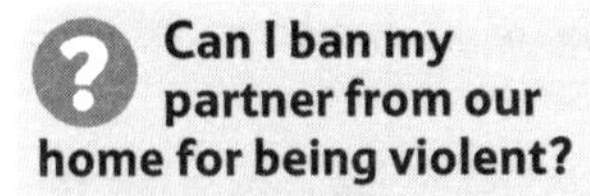

Can I ban my partner from our home for being violent?

Yes, by applying to the court for an occupation order. You must be able to prove that your partner has been violent or that you have suffered psychological harm.

It may be possible to exclude a person from the family home by applying to the court for an occupation order. If the person applying for the occupation order (known as the 'applicant') has either a legal or beneficial interest in the property, through ownership or a tenancy (see chapter 1 for further information), then he may find it relatively easy to obtain an occupation order against his cohabitant or former cohabitant. These orders, however, are usually only given by the court where there is evidence of violence or psychological harm, either to the parties or to their children if they remain living under the same roof. Occupation orders are usually granted for short periods only (often between three and six months), although they can be extended by the court. Under the existing law, same-sex cohabitants cannot obtain an occupation order.

Protection from harassment

Point of Law

Protection from Harassment Act 1997

If somebody is harassing you and you have not lived with them, you still may be able to obtain protection by applying for an injunction, usually by producing evidence of the harassment (e.g. photographs, videos or supporting evidence from a third party).

Your local County court can give you the form to make this application (as well as the other appropriate forms for any orders mentioned in this chapter) and will advise you about completing it. Alternatively, contact your local Citizens Advice Bureau or see www.courtservice.gov.uk. Proceedings may also be brought on a criminal law basis, which would involve you going to your local police and asking them to bring the proceedings for you.

The proposed new law

The Domestic Violence, Crime and Victims Bill 2003 is currently going through Parliament; it contains a number of proposed legislative reforms, with the general aim of strengthening the current law relating to domestic violence. Some of the provisions of this Bill can be summarised as follows:

A breach of a non-molestation order is to be a criminal offence

Under the existing law, a non-molestation order is punishable only as a contempt of court (i.e. by sending the offender to prison for a short period of time under civil law). Under the new law, a person who without good excuse breaches a non-molestation order will be treated as having committed a criminal offence which may make the offender liable to a term of imprisonment of up to five years, or a fine, or both. This will have the effect of making the offender a criminal, even though all the proceedings will have taken place in a civil court.

Definition of 'cohabitants'

This definition is to be changed to 'two persons who, although not married to each other, are living together as husband and wife or (if of the same sex) in an equivalent relationship'. The key development is the inclusion within the legislation of same-sex couples who currently do not count as cohabitants for the purpose of domestic violence legislation. Accordingly, under the new law, homosexual cohabitants will be able to apply for an occupation order.

The Bill will also extend the protection of the law of domestic violence to non-cohabiting couples who 'have or have had an intimate personal relationship which is or was of significant duration'. This means that people who have a relationship but do not live together may soon also have the protection of the law.

Common assault

The Bill states that an offender who is found guilty of common assault (i.e. where the victim sustained a minor injury) may be arrested, which means that an offender may find himself guilty of a criminal offence. This, in turn, will mean that more offenders are likely to be imprisoned.

Restraining orders, i.e. orders to prevent someone from doing something (usually assault)

The Bill contains a new power to make a restraining order against a defendant, even if he has been found not guilty.

There are various other provisions of the Bill, which are outside the scope of this book as they are more strictly related to criminal procedure. Perhaps the most important one is the creation of a new criminal offence of 'causing or allowing the death of a child or a vulnerable adult'. This proposed new offence is specifically aimed at situations of domestic abuse.

If you are a victim of domestic violence, you may find it helpful to gain support from one of the organisations listed in the 'Useful contacts' section.

CHAPTER 4

Splitting up

If your relationship goes wrong, you may not be able to rely on the law for protection as much as you may like: you cannot seek maintenance for yourself from your partner, nor can you make a claim over his pension or seek repayment of money you may have given to your partner by way of, for example, a housekeeping allowance. The division of the contents of the property you have occupied will depend on who paid for each item and whether any items were given by one of you to the other.

However, there are steps that you can take to protect yourself and your children, which are covered in this chapter. By far the best way to resolve your differences will be by way of agreement, as the law is a complex, uncertain and usually extremely costly way of resolving relationship breakdown problems. A better way of dealing with issues between you, if you are unable to do it directly, may be through mediation.

Mediation

Mediation is a process whereby a professional mediator assists a couple in reaching agreement. Mediators are totally impartial, but their skills enable them to help couples to overcome the obstacles which are preventing them from reaching agreement. Mediation can cover disputes relating to children and/or finances, but mediators often specialise in dealing with one or other of these areas.

If you think you may need a mediator to deal with both children and financial issues, make this clear at the outset so that you are given the right mediator for your problems. While mediators can give some legal advice, it will only be general and not specific to one of you because of their need to be neutral. It can therefore be a good idea to take legal advice about your rights before you enter into mediation so that you know the type of settlement you should try to achieve before you begin negotiating.

If you reach an agreement in mediation, this will not automatically be binding upon you. The mediator will therefore encourage you to take the proposed agreement to a lawyer so that he can draw up an agreement and advise you of any other legal steps you should take in order to make your agreement binding. This can be very important because if you do not take legal advice at this stage, one of you may go back on the agreement in the future. In addition, the correct legal steps to transfer property, such as houses or shares, may not have been correctly implemented, which may cause severe problems later on.

If you wish to find out more about mediation, contact the UK College of Family Mediators at the address given in the 'Useful contacts' section. They will be able to provide you with the names of suitable mediators in your area.

If you are unable to resolve matters either between yourselves or through mediation, Relate or another similar counselling organisation, then you may have to resort to the law. Before you do so, you will need to know what your legal position is. To help you find out, here are some typical problems relating to property and children that cohabitants are faced with when their relationship breaks down, with an explanation of the law and how it relates to those situations:

The property

The property you live in is rented and your name is not on the tenancy agreement

> **? Can my partner kick me out of our rented accommodation now that we've split up?**
>
> *If your name is not on the tenancy agreement, then normally, yes.*

Your position here is vulnerable. In certain circumstances (e.g. if your partner is being violent – see chapter 3), you may be able to apply for an occupation order, but more often than not you will find yourself simply packing your bags once your partner has asked you to leave. The reason for this is that he has the sole legal right to stay in the property.

In these circumstances, if you have children, the local authority has a duty to house you so it is wise to contact the local housing department of your local authority.

It may well also be appropriate for you to apply for the tenancy to be transferred into your sole name; for more information see chapter 1

The property you live in is owned by your partner

In certain circumstances, either direct financial contributions to the property or, in specific and limited circumstances, indirect contributions (e.g. payments towards household expenditure) may have given you a beneficial interest in the property. If so, you are not obliged to leave immediately. However, it may take some time to resolve the issue of how much your beneficial interest is worth.

In certain circumstances, you may be able to apply for an occupation order to remain in the property on a temporary basis while things are being sorted out. However, these are relatively rare so if you do not have a beneficial interest in the property, it is more likely that you are simply a 'bare licensee', which means that you are allowed to stay in the property only while the owner consents to it. As soon as your partner asks you to leave, legally speaking, you should vacate.

Obtaining a declaration about your beneficial interest in a property

Point of Law

Trusts of Land and Appointment of Trustees Act 1996

If you believe you have an interest in the property that is not properly reflected in the legal ownership, you can apply to the court for a 'declaration', which is a form of court order, as to the size of your beneficial interest in a property. This can be particularly useful if the property is owned by your partner and you believe that you have made a contribution to the property which may be reflected in financial terms. Once the court has made a declaration that you are entitled to a beneficial interest in the property, you can then apply for an order for sale from which you will receive a percentage of the net proceeds that the court deems to be the size of your beneficial interest.

Obtaining an order for sale

You can apply to a court using a claim form – which you can obtain from www.courtservice.gov.uk or from your local County court – for any property in which you and your partner have an interest to be sold, or to prevent your partner from forcing a sale. When you go to court in these circumstances a court can also order that either you or your partner can be prevented from occupying the property and it can even order that the person who has remained in the property pays compensation (sometimes called 'occupational rent') to the party who is excluded from it.

If it is not practical to order one of you to leave the property, the court can partition the land/property so that one of you occupies one part and the other another part or it can order the sale of part of it if this seems more appropriate.

When the court is considering whether or not to make an order, it has to take into account the following:

- The intention of the people who own the property. Therefore, if one person can show that the property was always intended to provide a home for the children of the family, the court may not order a sale until such time as the children are all grown up.
- The purpose for which the property was held. This could relate to either the property having been bought for the sake of the children or, alternatively, to house an elderly relative or for some other purpose.
- The welfare of any child who occupies or may be expected to occupy that property as his home. If there are children involved, therefore, the court is less likely to order a sale, although it may still order a sale in certain circumstances.
- The interests of any person who is owed money by an owner of the property who has registered the loan against the property. This may include a building society or bank that has the mortgage on the property which has not been paid and that wishes the property to be sold in order that the mortgage can be paid off.

So as you can see, the court is less likely to order a sale of the property where it is not in the interests of the children. However, this is not an overriding consideration and the court may still order a sale even where there are children in certain circumstances.

Concerning the contents of a property, see chapter 1 on items purchased jointly. Those items bought by or given to you personally will be treated as belonging to you. Although you can apply to the court to make orders regarding who owns other personal possessions and whether they should be sold, the court will very rarely wish to become involved in a dispute over these. By far the best way of dealing with this is to ensure that if you leave the property, you take those possessions that are very dear to you with you. It is rarely advisable to go to court over them.

The property you live in is owned by the two of you

As discussed in chapter 1, you will either own the property as joint tenants or as tenants in common. If you own it as joint tenants, then it is advisable that you sever the joint tenancy immediately because it is unlikely that you will want your share in the property to pass to your partner in the event that you die before him. Legal advice should be taken regarding severing a joint tenancy.

If you are forced to leave the property by reason of your partner's behaviour towards you, particularly if it is violent, then the law tends to take a lenient view regarding your obligation to pay your share of the mortgage and other outgoings on the property once you have vacated and is unlikely to order that you should pay your share of the mortgage after leaving. If, however, you are leaving entirely of your own free will, the courts tend to expect you to continue to pay your share of the mortgage and the outgoings that relate to the fabric of the property (e.g. Council Tax), as opposed to the bills that relate to the occupation of the property, such as electricity and gas.

? Do I still have to share the costs for running the property even though I've moved out?

If you've left of your own free will, the courts may still expect you to pay your share of the mortgage, taxes and repairs, etc. but not the bills involved for actually living in it.

Allowing someone else into the home

If your partner has allowed someone else in to occupy the property, then the law is very complex since the person he has allowed into the property is there with the permission of one owner but perhaps not with the permission of the other. The visitor, therefore, is not guilty of trespass and usually the only effective remedy of getting him out of the property is to force a sale. Therefore, when a trust deed detailing your issues regarding your property is being drafted (see chapter 1), it is often a good idea to record that one person will not invite anybody else to occupy the property (e.g. a new boyfriend or girlfriend) without the agreement of the other party, except in certain circumstances.

Can my ex-partner move his new lover into the family home without my permission?

Yes, and the only way you can get the lover out is to force your partner to sell the property.

Your partner will not agree to the property being sold and/or your partner will not agree how much of the proceeds of the sale you are entitled to

In this situation you will need legal advice about bringing court proceedings for an order for the sale of the property and/or an order regarding the division of the net proceeds from the sale of the property.

The children

You need to obtain child support from your partner

If your partner (i.e. the 'non-resident parent' who is not providing the main base for the children) lives in the UK or is employed by a UK company or in government service, then you, with the day-to-day care of the children, can make an application to the Child Support Agency for support from him for the children. The non-resident parent can also apply.

The formula to calculate how much support you will receive is now a relatively straightforward one: broadly speaking, a non-resident parent should pay 15 per cent of his net income ('net' being defined as his gross income less tax, National Insurance and pension contributions) for one child, 20 per cent for two children and 25 per cent for three children or more. This assessment is reduced by one-seventh for each overnight stay per week on average through the year that a child spends with his non-resident parent and also allows for new family members. For full details, contact the CSA helpline on the number given in the 'Useful contacts' section. The Child Support Agency is also responsible for enforcing assessments if a parent does not pay child maintenance.

You need financial help from your partner to house the children

Point of Law

Children Act 1989

If, after the separation, your children live with you and you do not have sufficient money either to house them or to provide them with the capital that they need, you can apply for an order against your partner either for a lump sum or for a property transfer order for the benefit of the children; these applications are made under Schedule 1 of the Children Act 1989. Be aware that you may only seek an order against your partner in relation to children that are his, not in relation to children from another relationship.

Often, this application is made to 'top up' the money or capital in a house that the parent looking after the children owns, either legally or beneficially, so that the parent can provide a proper home for the children while they are young. It works like this:

Val and Jo jointly own a property worth £200,000 as joint tenants. They split up and Val needs £150,000 to purchase a three-bedroom property for her and the two children. She can raise a mortgage of £30,000 so she applies for a lump sum of £20,000:

£100,000	Val's half share
£30,000	Mortgage
£20,000	Lump sum
£150,000	

These lump sum and property transfer orders must be given back to the person from whom they are obtained when the youngest child either reaches the age of 18 or ceases full-time education.

CHAPTER 5

Gay and lesbian rights

Gays and lesbians who live together have no special rights against each other at all. This means that the surviving partner of a gay or lesbian couple cannot gain pension rights (employment benefits are reserved only for married partners) and he may even be refused a hospital visit to see his seriously ill partner. This, however, is all soon to change.

In November 2003, the Government published a Civil Partnership Bill for the legal recognition of same-sex partnerships. This follows the publication of a consultation document by the Department of Trade and Industry in June 2003 entitled *Civil Partnership – A Framework for the Legal Recognition of Same-Sex Couples*. In this consultation document it was proposed that there should be the creation of a new legal status for same-sex couples who choose to register under a civil partnership scheme. The Bill provides that upon registration of the partnership, same-sex couples will have rights and responsibilities during and upon the dissolution of the relationship that mirror marriage and divorce.

If the Civil Partnership Bill becomes law, then the UK will be coming into line with eight European Union member states and some states in the United States, Canada and Australia which have already introduced some form of civil partnership registration scheme. The degree of rights attached to the different schemes varies and some allow heterosexual couples to opt into the scheme. However, in the UK, there are no plans as yet for heterosexual couples to be allowed to opt into it. The argument behind this is that heterosexual couples can marry if they choose to do so whereas same-sex couples cannot.

Under the proposed new law the following legal consequences will follow from registering a civil partnership:

- Joint treatment for income-related state benefits.
- Joint treatment for state pension benefits.
- The ability to gain parental responsibility for each other's children (at present only available to natural fathers).
- Recognition for immigration purposes.
- Exemption from testifying against each other in court (which puts gays and lesbians in the same position as married couples).

If the relationship breaks down, then the new law will provide for there to be some formal rights against property owned by a couple and it will allow for court orders to be made regarding residence and contact with children. In the event of the death of one partner, the new law will provide:

- the right to register the death of a partner for the purpose of obtaining the death certificate;
- the right to claim the survivor's pension;
- eligibility for bereavement benefits;
- compensation for fatal accidents or criminal injuries;
- recognition under the Inheritance Act and the intestacy rules;
- the right to be able to 'succeed' (i.e. take over) a tenancy.

At the time of going to press, the Bill is not complete and it may change substantially before it becomes law. For instance, there is very little detail in it about the pension rights that will be available. It appears that companies are not legally bound to recognise a civil partner's benefits in their pension schemes but all major civil service schemes will provide for partners to get full pension rights. In respect of the state pension scheme, same-sex couples will have to wait until 2010 to see full equality.

If the partnership breaks down, a couple will be entitled to apply for the court to decide how their assets will be divided up if they cannot reach an agreement between themselves. In addition, they will be able to apply for the partnership to be dissolved if they can show it has broken down irretrievably.

Insofar as heterosexual couples are concerned, the scheme will not be open to them. However, the Law Society and the Solicitors Family Law Association have both proposed that there should be new legalisation to provide a basic safety net of rights and responsibilities for all couples who cohabit; it is expected that within the next few years a new law may well be introduced for heterosexual couples which mirrors the Civil Partnership Bill.

? Does the law give any particular rights to people in same-sex relationships?

Not at present, but proposals have been made to change this.

CHAPTER 6

Benefits and taxation

Benefits

If you are a lone parent, it may be particularly important for you to take advantage of all the available benefits and tax credits. It is beyond the scope of this Pocket Law Guide to cover the whole range of benefits so instead we will take a look at three benefits or tax credits that are likely to be relevant following the end of an unmarried relationship.

Child Benefit

This benefit is paid to you if you are caring for children who are either under 16 years old or between 16 and 19 years old and in full-time study. It is payable for each child in your care. Presently £16.50 per week will be paid for the eldest child who qualifies and £11.05 will be paid per week for each other child. The benefit can be claimed by calling your local Child Benefit Office on 0845 302 1444 or, alternatively, it can be claimed online at www.inlandrevenue.gov.uk/childbenefit.

Child Tax Credit

Child Tax Credit is available to you if you look after one or more qualifying young people. You do not need to be working to claim it. A qualifying young person is:

- any child until 1 September following his or her 16th birthday;

- a young person older than 16 but under 19 who:
    - is in full-time education; or
    - has left full-time education but does not have a job or training place and has registered with the careers service; or
    - is not claiming Income Support or tax credits in his own right; or
    - is not serving a custodial sentence of four months or more which has been imposed by the court.

Child Tax Credit is made up of different elements and the amount you receive will therefore depend on your circumstances, including your income. To claim it, go to www.taxcredits.inlandrevenue.gov.uk or call the Tax Credits Helpline on 0845 300 3900.

Working Tax Credit

Working Tax Credit is available to you if you are in work (either as an employee or self-employed), you are paid for the work that you do and you expect to be working for at least four weeks. In addition, you need to be:

- aged 16 or over, usually working 16 hours or more per week and you are either looking after at least one child or you are disabled; or
- aged 25 or over and usually working at least 30 hours per week; or
- aged 50 or over and starting work after receiving certain benefits for at least six months and usually working at least 16 hours per week.

Again, Working Tax Credit is made up of various elements and the amount you receive will depend on your circumstances. Relevant factors include not only the amount you earn, but also the amount of hours you work per week (the tax credit usually increases if you work more than 30 hours per week), the fact that you are a lone parent and any amounts you spend on registered or approved childcare.

Many people do not realise that they are eligible to apply for tax credits. Both couples and lone parents may apply and the level of credit awarded will be based on the applicant's income (in the case of a couple, their combined income) for the previous tax year. However, any change of circumstances should lead to a fresh application being made for the amount of credits to be reviewed.

Taxation

The law relating to tax changes with every Budget, so it is impossible to keep this book up to date regarding taxation.

The main aspects of taxation and how it relates to those who live together is to bear in mind that there are no special rules benefiting cohabiting couples. This means that you are taxed as individuals and are not eligible for any extra personal allowances by virtue of the fact that you live together. In relation to Inheritance Tax, this puts you at a distinct disadvantage when compared to married couples. When a married person dies, he may leave the whole of his estate to his surviving spouse and no Inheritance Tax arises. When a partner in a cohabiting couple dies, his estate attracts Inheritance Tax even if he leaves it to his surviving partner.

? Are there any taxable advantages from living together?

No, and you are particularly at a disadvantage when it comes to Inheritance Tax. If you are married and your spouse dies, you do not have to pay tax on his estate whereas a partner does.

Appendices

Appendix 1: Sources of documents

Cohabitation Agreement
Draft your own based on the example in this Guide.

Enduring Power of Attorney
Lawpack's *Power of Attorney Kit*, available via www.tesco.com/legalstore.

Health Care Proxy
Available from your local hospital.

Last Will & Testament
Lawpack's *Last Will & Testament Kit*, available via www.tesco.com/legalstore.

Living Together Agreement
Draft your own based on the example in this Guide.

Living Will
Lawpack's *Living Will Form*, available via www.tesco.com/legalstore.

Non-Molestation and Occupation Order, FL401
Available from the Court Service's website www.courtservice.gov.uk or call 020 7189 2000.

Orders relating to children, Form C1
Available from the Court Service's website www.courtservice.gov.uk or call 020 7189 2000.

Parental Responsibility Agreement, C(PRA)
Available from the Court Service's website www.courtservice.gov.uk or call 020 7189 2000.

Trust Deed
Available from your conveyancing solicitor.

Appendix 2: Sample documents

Cohabitation Agreement

This Deed is made on 3 August 2004 between:

Tony Arthur Smith ('Tony') of 23 Chankly Bore, Zemmery Fidd, Dorset; and **Valerie Mary Judd** ('Val') of 23 Chankly Bore, Zemmery Fidd, Dorset.

Whereas:

1. a) We wish to enter into an Agreement which regulates our rights and obligations to each other.

b) We have taken independent legal advice.[1]

c) We have disclosed to each other our respective financial positions (schedules of our respective income, assets and liabilities are attached).[2]

d) We intend the terms of this Agreement to be legally binding.

e) We are entering into this Agreement of our own free will and have not been put under any pressure to sign it.

2. The terms of this Agreement:

a) are effective from the date written above;

b) are severable;[3]

c) are to be interpreted by the Courts of England and Wales which courts we intend to have jurisdiction in relation to it.

[1] It is important for both parties to have received independent legal advice before they enter into an Agreement. Any Agreement is then less likely to be rejected by the court.

[2] Do not forget to prepare these.

[3] So that if any part of the Agreement is declared invalid, the remaining clauses will remain valid.

Cohabitation Agreement (continued)

3. 23 Chankly Bore, Zemmery Fidd, Dorset

a) This is to be purchased/transferred into our joint names and held by us as tenants in common so that if either of us dies, that person's share will be dealt with in accordance with that person's Will/law of intestacy.

b) In the alternative, it is to be held by us as joint tenants so if either of us were to die, his/her share will pass automatically to the survivor regardless of any Will, etc. [4]

c) The purchase price of the property was [£] which we raised as follows:

(i) [£] by way of a mortgage from [ ] Building Society;

(ii) contribution towards the deposit from Tony of [£];

(iii) contribution towards the deposit from Val of [£].

d) the following policies are linked to the mortgage and in the event of death of either of us the proceeds will be paid over to reduce the mortgage account:

Name of insurance company: __________

Policy no: __________

Life assured: __________

Death benefit: __________

% in the policy owned by Tony: __________

% in the policy owned by Val:

[4] Refer to the beginning of chapter 1 regarding the difference between joint tenants and tenants in common. It is important to delete which is applicable here.

Cohabitation Agreement (continued)

(i) Tony will pay the premiums on the following policies: [LIST]

(ii) Val will pay the premiums on the following policies: [LIST]

(iii) We will jointly contribute towards the policies on the following percentage basis as follows: [LIST]

THIS DEED evidences that we have agreed as follows:

4. **Shares in 23 Chankly Bore, Zemmery Fidd, Dorset**

   a) Tony will own [ ]% of the property and Val will own the remaining [ ]%; [5]

   b) We will contribute towards any necessary repairs or improvements to 23 Chankly Bore, Zemmery Fidd, Dorset in these proportions. [6]

5. **Outgoings**

   We will contribute towards the outgoings of the property in these proportions [OR STATE OTHERWISE IF APPROPRIATE]. These outgoings are as follows:

   - Buildings insurance
   - Council tax
   - Service charges

   [CONTINUE TO LIST HERE]

6. **Other outgoings on 23 Chankly Bore, Zemmery Fidd, Dorset**

   a) Unless we agree something else in writing or a

[5] Different percentages are only applicable to a tenancy in common. To protect your tenancy in common, ensure your conveyancing solicitor registers it at the Land Registry for you as a 'restriction'.

[6] If you keep to the same percentages for all contributions towards repairs, mortgage payments and outgoings that relate to the property (as opposed to outgoings that relate to the occupation of the property such as gas and electricity), then it will be easier to calculate exactly what you both own.

Cohabitation Agreement (continued)

court makes an order that is different, we agree to make equal contributions towards all of the utilities on the property namely:

- Gas
- Electricity
- Water rates
- Telephone
- Oil

b) If either of us leaves the property permanently and the other remains in occupation, then we will continue to pay the outgoings listed above at 6(a) in the following percentages:

Tony [ ]%

Val [ ]%

for the period of three months following the separation date.

The one remaining in occupation will pay all of the aforementioned outgoings three months and one day after the date of separation until he/she permanently leaves the property.

From the date of separation we will contribute to the mortgage instalments as follows:

Tony [ ]%

Val [ ]%

In the event that one party does not meet his/her prescribed percentage of the mortgage instalments, then upon the sale of the property, account will be taken of this so that the party who has paid more than his/her prescribed share of the mortgage instalments will be fully compensated.

Cohabitation Agreement (continued)

c) After the date of our separation we will continue to pay the premiums on the policies in the shares prescribed above at paragraph 3(d).

7. Improvements

We agree:

a) to carry out any improvements, including repairs, which increase the value of 23 Chankly Bore, Zemmery Fidd, Dorset only by agreement between us or as recommended by a chartered surveyor appointed (and paid for) by us together (and if we cannot agree then as appointed by the President for the time being of the Royal Institute of Chartered Surveyors);

b) to pay for equally/in the proportions in which we own 23 Chankly Bore, Zemmery Fidd, Dorset the cost and work involved;

c) that in the event that this is not done and neither of us pays a greater sum, then upon the sale of the property or transfer of the property in accordance with the terms of this Deed the party who paid for the improvement shall be entitled to seek repayment and to charge interest at 3% interest per annum above Bank of England base rate on the sum paid.

8. Sale or transfer of the property

a) Within the period of three months following the date of separation, one of us may offer to buy out the other's interest in it at an agreed price. In order to agree the price, three local estate agents will be asked to give valuations for the property but in the event that the value still cannot be agreed, then we will request the President of the Institute of

Cohabitation Agreement (continued)

Chartered Surveyors, for the time being, to nominate a local valuer to value the property and that valuation will become binding upon us. Our respective shares in the property shall then be calculated in accordance with that value. The cost of the valuation will be borne equally between us.

b) In the event that an offer is made by one of us in accordance with paragraph 8(a) above, then all best endeavours must be made to ensure that the completion of the purchase of the other party's share is completed within six months of the date of separation.

9. In the event that one of us does not purchase the other's share in the property, in accordance with paragraphs 8(a) and 8(b) above, then we will market the property as agreed and in default of agreement we will:

a) invite immediately no fewer than one estate agent each to consider the marketing strategy to be employed to dispose of the property at the best price reasonably obtainable within the period of three months from the date of instruction;

b) instruct each of the agents to report to us both simultaneously within one week in writing on the strategy it each recommends;

c) market the property in accordance with the proposed strategies;

d) require each of the respective agents to report to us simultaneously on each inspection arranged at the property and any offer made for the purchase of it;

e) market the property pending exchange of contracts;

Cohabitation Agreement (continued)

f) use [NAME FIRM OF SOLICITORS HERE] if we do not agree on the firm of solicitors to use.

10. The net sale of proceeds of the property

From the gross sale proceeds of the sale of the property, we will pay:

a) the estate agent's fees or other marketing expenses;

b) the legal costs of sale;

c) whatever is required to pay off the mortgage secured on the property.

The balance will be divided between us in the proportions set out at paragraph 4 above. In the event that the gross sale proceeds of the property are not enough to meet all of the above, then we will each pay one half of the shortfall at least seven days prior to the completion of the sale to the solicitor conducting the conveyancing.

11. Dealing with the proceeds of the policies

The policies which are held in our respective sole names shall be retained by the policyholders. The joint policies shall be divided between us in accordance with the contributions made by us towards the premiums, and in the event that the said premiums are paid from our joint account, equally between us. We hereby agree to co-operate with each other in relation to the sale or surrender of the policies in order to obtain the best price achievable.

12. New home

In the event that we sell 23 Chankly Bore, Zemmery Fidd, Dorset and purchase another property, we will enter into a new Agreement at the time of purchase, setting out our interest in that property.

Cohabitation Agreement (continued)

13. Further promises about the property

a) Neither of us will allow any other person in to occupy the property unless the period of three months referred to in paragraph 6(b) above has expired and it is necessary for the party remaining in occupation to obtain financial assistance from another person in order to meet the mortgage payments and associated policy payments in full.

b) Neither of us will do anything that makes the building or contents insurance cover lapse or terminate.

14. Bank accounts

a) We will maintain the following joint accounts: [LIST HERE]

b) We will make equal contributions to the aforesaid joint accounts on the first of each month until the first happens of:

(i) a new Agreement;

(ii) either of us dying;

(iii) three months after the separation date.

c) We will discharge all outgoings that relate to the occupation of the property from Account Number [ ].[7]

d) We will make no unreasonable withdrawal from any of the joint accounts without the agreement of the other.

e) We will co-operate with each other in relation to the closing of the aforesaid joint accounts immediately upon three months after the date of separation.

[7] For example, gas, electricity, water rates, telephone, etc.

Cohabitation Agreement (continued)

f) If either of us dies, the other will become entitled to a credit balance on any of the joint accounts, but may seek a one-half contribution towards any debit balance from any other assets in the deceased's estate.

15. Things we will own in the future

a) Gifts (including inheritances) will belong to the person who receives them.

b) Any asset will be owned by the person who paid for it.

c) In the event that an asset is purchased out of the joint account, then it is to be owned equally and upon separation it shall be agreed which party shall retain the item and he/she will compensate the other by paying one-half of the 'as new' price to the other.

d) In the event that a gift is made to both of us by friends or family of one of us, then the person whose family or friends gave the gift shall retain the item in the event of separation or death.

e) In the event of our separation, unless one of us can release the other from any joint hire purchase liability, then any item on hire purchase or similar will be sold and we will pay the proceeds towards the hire purchase account and take such steps as shall be required to discharge equally any remaining balance to include, if necessary, taking out a loan in our sole names.

16. Personal items

We will each be entitled to remove from the property upon the separation date:

Cohabitation Agreement (continued)

a) our personal possessions to include clothing, personal jewellery and things relating to our work (regardless of who paid for them);

b) things we each owned prior to the dating of this Deed;

c) gifts we have personally received (to include inheritances);

d) things that Tony has purchased from [ ];

e) things that Val has purchased from [ ].

17. The remainder of the contents shall be divided as though they are jointly owned. A coin will be tossed in front of an independent witness to determine who shall retain the item and which party shall pay the relevant proportion of the new value to the person who loses the item.

We have signed this document and had it witnessed because we intend it to be a Deed and be binding upon us:

Signed by TONY ARTHUR SMITH

....

In the presence of

.... (witness's signature)

Witness's name....................................

Witness's address ....

....

....

Witness's occupation ....

Cohabitation Agreement (continued)

Signed by VALERIE MARY JUDD

....

In the presence of

.... (witness's signature)

Witness's name....................................

Witness's address ....

....

....

Witness's occupation ....

Living Together Agreement

This Living Together Agreement is made between:

Tony Arthur Smith ('Tony') of 23 Chankly Bore, Zemmery Fidd, Dorset and **Valerie Mary Judd** ('Val') of 23 Chankly Bore, Zemmery Fidd, Dorset.

1. We cohabit/intend to cohabit by which we mean that:
   - we will live together as a family unit and hold ourselves out as being a family;
   - we will share our lives together;
   - we will support each other emotionally;
   - we will be honest to each other;
   - we will be sexually faithful to each other.
2. We have the following children:
   a) Alfred Smith;
   b) Zara Judd;
   c) Austin Smith-Judd.
3. Alfred is Tony's child by his first marriage and Zara is a child by Valerie's previous relationship. It is agreed that they are to be treated as children of the family unit and that both Tony and Val can discipline each other's child, as appropriate, but under no circumstances may they use physical force against the other's child.
4. In the case of Austin, who is the child of both Tony and Val, it is agreed that they have equal rights, duties and responsibilities towards him which is reflected in the Parental Responsibility Agreement that Val and Tony have entered into dated 3 August 2004.
5. Val understands that Tony does not get on well with her mother and likewise Tony understands that Val likes her to come and stay, particularly to help with the care of the children during the school holidays. As a compromise,

Living Together Agreement (continued)

therefore, it is agreed that Val's mother will not come and stay for any longer than three days at a time and on no more than three separate occasions in each year. On each occasion, Val must ask Tony at least two weeks prior to her mother's arrival if her mother may come and Tony will not unreasonably withhold his consent.

6. Val understands that Tony is passionate about Bedford United. Tony recognises, however, that when he goes to matches this creates additional work for Val who is left to look after the children on her own. Tony therefore agrees that he will not go to any more than four matches in any one season. The cost of attending those matches will be borne solely by Tony and will not be paid for out of the joint account. Tony will not stay overnight at his friend Bill's house after attending these matches.

7. Tony appreciates that Val is a member of the Elim Pentecostal Church and he will not prevent Val from taking the children to Church every Sunday morning. Likewise, Val will not pressurise Tony into accompanying them.

8. In the event that Tony and Val have difficulties in their relationship, they both promise to discuss them with each other at the earliest opportunity. Should either Tony or Val wish to refer their difficulties to an organisation, counsellor or therapist, the other will not withhold his/her agreement to attend at least the first three sessions with that organisation/individual.

9. Val and Tony have agreed that all of the children, Alfred, Zara and Austin, will attend the Rudolf Steiner School in Borset for as long as Tony's mother is willing to pay their respective school fees.

10. Val acknowledges that Tony has higher standards of cleanliness and home neatness than she has.

Living Together Agreement (continued)

Commencing 1 September 2004 Val and then Tony shall, on a monthly basis, alternate as the inspector of household work for cleanliness and neatness. On the month when Tony is inspector, Val will conform to his standards and Tony will conform to the standards set by Val during her month.

11. Tony will not play his saxophone after 9.30pm in the evening and on no more than three nights a week.

[***Since a Living Together Agreement is not a legally binding document, you can then put in numbered paragraphs concerning any matters you consider appropriate. Issues commonly covered include the following:***

1. ***Children***
   a) ***Registering the birth***
   b) ***The child's surname***
   c) ***Care of the child including discipline***
   d) ***Religion***
   e) ***Expected education***
   f) ***Childcare***
2. ***Personal relations***
   a) ***Contraception***
   b) ***Sexual relations***
3. ***The prospect of marriage***
4. ***Housekeeping***]

Signed

....

Tony Arthur Smith

Signed

....

Valerie Mary Judd

Dated ....

Parental Responsibility Agreement

Parental Responsibility Agreement

Section 4(1)(b) Children Act 1989

Keep this form in a safe place
Date recorded at the Principal Registry of the Family Division

Read the notes on the other side before you make this agreement.

This is a Parental Responsibility Agreement regarding

the Child *Name*

Boy or Girl *Date of birth* *Date of 18th birthday*

Between
the Mother *Name*

Address

and the Father *Name*

Address

We declare that we are the mother and father of the above child and we agree that the child's father shall have parental responsibility for the child (in addition to the mother having parental responsibility).

Signed (**Mother**)	Signed (**Father**)
Date	Date

Certificate of witness

The following evidence of identity was produced by the person signing above:	The following evidence of identity was produced by the person signing above:
Signed in the presence of: *Name of Witness*	Signed in the presence of: *Name of Witness*
Address	*Address*
Signature of Witness	*Signature of Witness*
[A Justice of the Peace] [Justices' Clerk] [An Officer of the Court authorised by the judge to administer oaths]	[A Justice of the Peace] [Justices' Clerk] [An Officer of the Court authorised by the judge to administer oaths]

C(PRA) - w3 (9.01) *On behalf of The Court Service*

Parental Responsibility Agreement (continued)

Notes about the Parental Responsibility Agreement

Read these notes before you make the agreement.

About the Parental Responsibility Agreement

The making of this agreement will affect the legal position of the mother and the father. You should both seek legal advice before you make the Agreement. You can obtain the name and address of a solicitor from the Children Panel (020 7242 1222) or from

- your local family proceedings court, or county court
- a Citizens Advice Bureau
- a Law Centre
- a local library.

You may be eligible for public funding.

When you fill in the Agreement

Please use black ink (the Agreement will be copied). Put the name of one child only. If the father is to have parental responsibility for more than one child, fill in a separate form for each child. **Do not sign the Agreement.**

When you have filled in the Agreement

Take it to a local family proceedings court, or county court, or the Principal Registry of the Family Division (the address is below).

A justice of the peace, a justices' clerk, or a court official who is authorised by the judge to administer oaths, will witness your signature and he or she will sign the certificate of the witness.

To the mother: When you make the declaration you will have to prove that you are the child's mother so take to the court the child's full birth certificate.
You will also need evidence of your identity showing a photograph and signature (for example, a photocard, official pass or passport).

To the father: You will need evidence of your identity showing a photograph and signature (for example, a photocard, official pass or passport).

When the Certificate has been signed and witnessed

Make 2 copies of the other side of this form. You do not need to copy these notes.
Take, or send, this form and the copies to **The Principal Registry of the Family Division, First Avenue House, 42-49 High Holborn, London, WC1V 6NP.**

The Registry will record the Agreement and keep this form. The copies will be stamped and sent back to each parent at the address on the Agreement. The Agreement will not take effect until it has been received and recorded at the Principal Registry of the Family Division.

Ending the Agreement

Once a parental responsibility agreement has been made it can only end

- by an order of the court made on the application of any person who has parental responsibility for the child
- by an order of the court made on the application of the child with leave of the court
- when the child reaches the age of 18.

C(PRA) (Notes)

Appendix 3: Useful contacts

British Association of Psychotherapists
37 Mapesbury Road
London NW2 4HJ
Tel: 020 8452 9823
Email: mail@bap-psychotherapy.org
Website: www.bap-psychotherapy.org

Child Support Agency
PO Box 55
Brierley Hill
West Midlands DY5 1YL
Tel: 0845 713 3133
Website: www.csa.gov.uk

Families need Fathers
132 Curtain Road
London EC2A 3AR
Tel: 0870 760 7496
Website: www.fnf.org.uk

HM Land Charges Registry
(for unregistered land)
Drakes Hill Court
Burrington Way
Plymouth PL5 3LP
Tel: 01752 635 600

HM Land Registry
32 Lincoln's Inn Fields
London WC2A 3PH
Tel: 020 7917 8888
Website: www.landreg.gov.uk

Inland Revenue
Tel: 0845 070 3703
Website: www.inlandrevenue.gov.uk

Law Society
113 Chancery Lane
London WC2A 1PL
Tel: 020 7242 1222
Website: www.lawsociety.org.uk

Men's Aid
Email: support@mensaid.org
Website: www.mensaid.org

National Association of Citizens Advice Bureaux
115 Pentonville Road
London N1 9LZ
Tel: 020 7833 2181
Website: www.nacab.org.uk

National Council for One Parent Families
255 Kentish Town Road
London NW5 1TL
Tel: 020 7428 5400
Website: www.oneparentfamilies.org.uk

National Family and Parenting Institute
430 Highgate Studios
53–79 Highgate Road
London NW5 1TL
Tel: 020 7424 3460
Website: www.nfpi.org

Principal Registry of the Family Division
The Children's Section (Room 2.11)
1st Avenue
42–49 High Holborn
London WC1V 6NP
Tel: 020 7947 7461/6939

Refuge
2-8 Maltravers Street
London WC2R 3EE
Tel: 0808 200 0247
Website: www.refuge.org.uk

Relate
Herbert Gray College
Little Church Street
Rugby CV21 3AP
Tel: 01788 573 241
Website: www.relate.org.uk

Solicitors Family Law Association
(*for solicitors and mediators*)
PO Box 302
Orpington BR6 8QX
Tel: 01689 850 227
Website: www.sfla.co.uk

UK College of Family Mediators
24–32 Stephenson Way
London NW1 2HX
Tel: 020 7391 9162
Website: www.ukcfm.co.uk

Women's Aid
PO Box 391
BS99 7WS
Tel: 0808 200 0247
Website: www.womensaid.org.uk

Index

abduction, of children 20
access orders (became contact orders) 26
accounts, joint 6–7
Adoption and Children Act 2002 21
age
    attitudes to partnerships and vi
    children's age and wishes, court orders and 24–5
    prevalence and vi
agreements 1–2 see also individual terms
assault 30–1
attitudes to partnerships, age and vi

bank accounts, joint 6–7
bare licences 3, 35
benefits
    Child Benefit 45
    Child Tax Credit 45–6, 47
    Working Tax Credit 46–7
bill payments 8, 38
birth registration
    IVF and 18
    parents on 17–18
    statutory declarations 17–18
Births and Deaths Registration Act 1953 17–18

Child Abduction Act 1984 20
Child Benefit 45
child support 21, 39
Child Support Agency 21, 39-40
Child Tax Credit 45–6, 47

children vi
    abduction 20
    birth registration 17–18
    Child Benefit 45
    Child Tax Credit 45–6, 47
    court orders for 4
        children's age, wishes and 24–5
        contact orders 26
        parental responsibility agreements 22–3, 25, 64–5
        prohibited steps orders 26
        residence orders 25–6
        scope 24
        specific issue orders 26
    financial arrangements for 21, 39–40
    intestacy on 13–14
    negotiations for 24
    parental responsibility for 19–21
    tenancies on 4
    welfare 18–19
        housing 35, 36–7
    Wills on 14
Children Act 1989 18–19, 40
civil partnership proposals
    on pensions 42–3
    on protection following death 42
    scope 41–2, 43
cohabitation agreements 8
    marriage and 9
    sample 50–60
    trust deeds and 5
    updating 9
common law marriages vii
contact orders (was access orders) 26
Court of Protection 11
credit cards, joint 7–8
custody orders (became residence orders) 25–6

death 1, 42

of dependants, from domestic violence 31
inequity of survivors 4–5, 12–13
intestacy 13–14
Wills 2, 12, 13, 14, 15
debts, joint 7–8
dependants
children *see* children
death, from domestic violence 31
doctrine of necessity 11
domestic violence
assault 30–1
death of dependants 31
increased protection from 27
Domestic Violence, Crime and Victims Bill 2003 29–31
non-molestation orders 28, 30
occupation orders 28–9, 35
prevalence 27
protection from harassment 29
restraining orders 31
Domestic Violence, Crime and Victims Bill 2003 29
on assault 30–1
on death of dependants 31
on definition of cohabitants 30
on non-molestation orders 30
on restraining orders 31
scope 30

employment, Working Tax Credit 46–7
Enduring Power of Attorney (EPA) 10–11
estates *see individual terms*

families
children *see* children
intestacy on 13–14
Family Law Act 1996 4, 27
fathers see children
financial arrangements 1

benefits 45–7
bill payments 8, 37, 38
for children 21, 39–40
intestacy on 13–14
joint accounts 6–7
joint debts 7–8
joint purchases 7
pensions 12, 42–3
property sales 8, 36–7, 39
taxation 45–7
Wills on 2, 13, 14, 15

gay and lesbian couples
civil partnership proposals
on pensions 42–3
on protection following death 42
scope 41–2, 43
court orders for 43
inequity 41, 43
on occupation orders 29
General Power of Attorney (GPA) 11

Hague Convention 20
harassment, protection from 29
healthcare proxy appointment forms 12
homes see property
Human Fertilisation and Embryology Act 1990 18

illness
doctrine of necessity 11
Enduring Power of Attorney 10–11
General Power of Attorney 11
healthcare proxy appointment forms 12
Living Wills 12
next of kin 11–12
inequity vii, 1 *see also individual terms*
Inheritance (Provision for Family and Dependants) Act 1975 13

Inheritance Tax 47
intestacy 13–14 see also Wills
IVF, birth registration and 18

joint bank accounts 6–7
joint debts 7–8
joint purchases 7
joint tenants 4, 38–9

knowledge 1

law of equity 2–3
lesbian and gay couples
  civil partnership proposals
    on pensions 42–3
    on protection following death 42
    scope 41–2, 43
  court orders for 43
  inequity 41, 43
    on occupation orders 29
living together agreements 9–10
  sample 61–3
Living Wills 12
loans 37
local authorities, on housing for children 35
lump sum orders 39–40

marriage
  cohabitation agreements and 9
  common law marriages vii
mediation
  for children 24
  scope 33–4
mental incapacity
  Enduring Power of Attorney and 10–11
  General Power of Attorney and 11
molestation 28
mothers *see* children

next of kin
    healthcare proxy appointment forms 12
    inequity 11–12
no order principle 24
non-molestation orders 28, 30

occupation orders 28–9, 35
occupational rent 36

parental responsibility
    on child support 21
    claims 19–20
    inequity 19–20, 21
    parental responsibility agreements 22–3, 25, 64–5
    scope 19
    on travel outside jurisdiction 20
parental responsibility agreements 25
    court process 22, 23
    identification for 22–3
    limitations 22
    sample 64–5
parents *see* children
payments, bills 8, 37, 38
pensions 12, 42–3
Principal Registry 23
prohibited steps orders 26
property 1
    bare licences 3, 35
    beneficial ownership 35
        declarations on 36
        inequity 2–3
        scope 2
        by trust deeds 3, 5–6
    bill payments 8, 37, 38
    cohabitation agreements on 8
    ex-partner's visitors occupying 38
    housing for children 35, 36–7
    occupation orders 28–9, 35

partitions, court orders 36
property transfer orders 39–40
registered ownership 2
by transfer 3
sales 8
court orders 36–7, 39
shares in ownership 4–5
limitations 37–8
tenancies 4, 35
property transfer orders 39–40
Protection from Harassment Act 1997 29
psychotherapy, for children 24
purchases, joint 7

renting
occupational rent 36
tenancies 4, 35
residence orders (was custody orders) 25–6
restraining orders 31
right of survivorship 4, 7

separation
on children 35, 37, 40
gay and lesbian couples 42, 43
inequity vii, 1, 33
mediation on 33–4
on property 4, 35–40
trust deeds 5–6
specific issue orders 26
sperm donation 22
spouses
intestacy on 13–14
Wills on 13
statutory declarations 17–18
store cards, joint 7–8

taxation
Child Tax Credit 45–6, 47

Inheritance Tax 47
scope 47
Working Tax Credit 46–7
tenancies
on children 4
inequity 35
by transfer 4
tenants
joint 4, 37–8
tenants in common 4–5
by transfer 4
tenants in common 4–5
travel, children 20
trust deeds 3
cohabitation agreements and 5
scope 5–6
Trusts of Land and Appointment of Trustees Act 1996 36

violence, domestic
assault 30–1
death of dependants 31
increased protection from 27
Domestic Violence, Crime and Victims Bill 2003 29–31
non-molestation orders 28, 30
occupation orders 28–9, 35
prevalence 27
protection from harassment 29
restraining orders 31
vulnerability vii, 1 *see also individual terms*

Wills 2, 15
on children 14
inequity 13
Living Wills 12
primacy 14
on spouses 13
Working Tax Credit 46–7